PRESENTED TO:

_____

FROM:

_____

WILLARD F. HARLEY, JR.

I CHERISH YOU

Words of wisdom from
His Needs, Her Needs

THE HUSBAND AND WIFE

WHO COMMIT THEMSELVES TO MEET EACH

OTHER'S NEEDS WILL LAY A FOUNDATION

FOR LIFELONG HAPPINESS IN A MARRIAGE

THAT IS DEEPER AND MORE SATISFYING THAN

THEY EVER DREAMED POSSIBLE.

I wrote this book for those of you who want to be happily married. Whether you are planning for marriage, are newly married, or have been married for many years, you can learn to have a happy marriage if you become aware of each other's emotional needs and learn to meet them.

When a man and woman marry, they share high expectations. They commit themselves to meeting certain intense and intimate needs in each other on an *exclusive* basis. Each agrees to "forsake all others," giving each other the exclusive right to meet these intimate needs.

WHEN A MAN AND WOMAN MARRY, THEY SHARE HIGH EXPECTATIONS OF EACH OTHER.

So to build a relationship that sustains romance and increases intimacy and closeness year after year, you need to know each other's basic needs and how to meet them.

When a husband and wife come to me for help, my first goal is to help them identify their most important emotional needs. Over the years, I have repeatedly asked the question, "What could your spouse do for you that would make you the happiest?" Most responses can be classified into the ten emotional needs you'll read about in this book.

Obviously the way to keep a husband and wife happily married is for each of them to meet the needs that are most important to the other.

"EACH PERSON IS UNIQUE"

But that is a difficult assignment. Because when asked to prioritize their needs, most men list them one way and women the opposite way.

But pay careful attention to this next point: *Each person is unique*. And while women *usually* pick a particular five emotional needs as most important and men usually pick the other five as most important, you may pick any of the ten as most important to *you*. I've identified the most important needs of the average man and the average woman, but I can't identify *your* most important emotional needs. You need to do that as you read the rest of this book.

Figuratively speaking, I believe each of us has a Love Bank. It contains many different accounts, one for each person we know. Each person makes either deposits or withdrawals whenever we interact with him or her. Pleasurable interactions cause deposits, and painful interactions cause withdrawals.

As life goes on the accounts in my Love Bank fluctuate. Some acquaintances build sizable deposits. Others remain in the black but have small balances because of fewer interactions with me. A third group has still smaller balances because my experiences with them are mixed, sometimes pleasant, sometimes painful.

Other people go into the red with me. They cause me more pain than pleasure. I never feel good when I think of them, and I do not want to see them or be with them. Their accounts at my Love Bank are overdrawn.

We affect each other emotionally with almost every encounter. The accumulation of positive and negative experiences determines our emotional reaction to those we know—including your spouse.

Successful marriages require skill—skill in caring for the one you promised to cherish throughout life. Good intentions are not enough. *This book will educate you in the care of your spouse.* Once you have learned its lessons, your spouse will find you irresistible, a condition that is essential to a happy and successful marriage.

The husband and wife who commit themselves to meet each other's needs will lay a foundation for lifelong happiness in a marriage that is deeper and more satisfying than they ever dreamed possible.

YOU CAN HAVE A HAPPY MARRIAGE
IF YOU LEARN TO BECOME AWARE
OF EACH OTHER'S NEEDS AND LEARN
TO MEET THEM.

One
AFFECTION

THE FIRST THING SHE CAN'T DO WITHOUT

EVERY MARRIAGE SHOULD HAVE AN

ATMOSPHERE THAT SAYS,

"I REALLY LOVE YOU AND

I KNOW YOU LOVE ME."

*T*o most women affection symbolizes security, protection, comfort, and approval, vitally important commodities in their eyes. When a husband shows his wife affection, he sends the following messages:

- I'll take care of you and protect you. You are important to me, and I don't want anything to happen to you.
- I'm concerned about the problems you face, and I am with you.
- I think you've done a good job, and I'm so proud of you.

A hug can say any and all of the above. Men need to understand how strongly women need these affirmations. *For the typical wife, there can hardly be enough of them.*

Obviously a man can display affection in other ways that can be equally important to a woman. A greeting card or a note expressing love and care can simply but effectively communicate the same emotions. Don't forget that all-time favorite—a bouquet of flowers. Women, almost universally, love to receive flowers. Occasionally I meet a man who likes to receive them, but most do not. For most women, however, flowers send a powerful message of love and concern.

An invitation to dinner also signals affection. It is a way of saying, "You don't need to do what you ordinarily do for me. I'll treat you instead. You are special to me, and I want to show you how much I love you."

Jokes abound on how after the wedding a wife has to find her own way in and out of cars, houses, restaurants, and so on. But a sensitive husband opens the door for his wife at

"I LOVE YOU AND CARE ABOUT YOU"

every opportunity—another way to say, "I love you and care about you."

Holding hands is a time-honored and effective sign of affection. Walks after dinner, back rubs, phone calls, and conversations with thoughtful and loving expressions all add units to the Love Bank. As more than one song has said, "There are a thousand ways to say I love you."

From a woman's point of view, affection is the essential cement of her relationship with a man. Without it, she feels alienated from her mate. With it she becomes tightly bonded to him.

When I go on a trip, I often find little notes Joyce has packed among my clothes. She is telling me she loves me, of course, but the notes send another message as well. Joyce would like to get the same little notes from me, and I have tried to leave such notes behind—on her pillow, for example—when I go out of town.

My needs for protection, approval, and care are not the same as hers, nor are they met in similar ways. I've had to discover these differences and act accordingly. For example, when we walk through a shopping center, it is important to her that we hold hands, something that would not occur to me naturally or automatically. She has encouraged me to take her hand, and I'm glad to do so, because I know she enjoys that and it says something she wants to hear.

Almost all men need some instruction in how to become more affectionate. In most marriages, a man's wife can become his best teacher, if he approaches her for help in the right way. She can help by making a list of those signs of care that mean the most to her.

To get you started, here are a few habits that go a long way toward helping you become an affectionate husband.

- Hug and kiss your wife every morning while you are still in bed.
- Tell her that you love her while you're having breakfast together.
- Kiss her before you leave for work.
- Call her during the day to see how she is doing.
- Bring her flowers as a surprise (be sure to include a card that expresses your love for her).
- Gifts for special occasions (birthday, anniversary, Christmas, Mother's Day, and Valentine's Day) should be sentimental, not practical.

MAKE A LIST OF THE SIGNS OF CARE THAT MEAN THE MOST TO HER.

- After work, call her before you leave for home, so that she can know when to expect you.
- When you arrive home from work, give her a hug and kiss and spend a few minutes talking to her about how her day went.
- Help with the dishes after dinner.
- Hug and kiss her every night before you go to sleep.

SEX BEGINS WITH AFFECTION

Affection is the environment of the marriage while sex is an event. Affection is a way of life, a canopy that covers and protects a marriage. It's a direct and convincing expression of love that gives the event of sex a more appropriate context. Most women need affection before sex means much to them.

Because men tend to translate affection into sex so readily, I try to teach a husband to make affection a non-sexual way of relating to his spouse. Whenever he and his spouse come together, a big hug and kiss should be routine. In fact, almost every interaction between them should include affectionate words and gestures. I believe every marriage should have an atmosphere that says, "I really love you and I know you love me."

In most cases, a woman needs to feel a oneness with her husband before she has sex with him. A couple achieves this feeling through the exchange of affection and undivided attention.

When it comes to sex and affection, you can't have one without the other. Most of the women I've counseled crave affection. I try to help their husbands understand the pleasure women feel when this need is met. Although they're not the same as those experienced during sex, they form a vital part of a romantic relationship. Without it, a woman's sexual experience is incomplete.

> WHEN IT COMES TO SEX AND AFFECTION, YOU CAN'T HAVE ONE WITHOUT THE OTHER.

A woman's need for affection is her deepest emotional need.

Two

SEXUAL FULFILLMENT

THE FIRST THING HE CAN'T DO WITHOUT

HE TRUSTS HER

TO MEET HIS SEXUAL NEED.

*B*efore we married, Jim was so romantic and affectionate—a regular Don Juan. Now he seems more like Attila the Hun."

"When John wants sex, he wants it right now. He doesn't care how I feel; all he cares about is satisfying himself."

When I hear wives make remarks like these, I understand how disillusioned they must feel. At one time men who knew how to give them affection swept them off their feet. But now that they

ONCE MARRIED, MANY MEN THINK AFFECTION IS UNNECESSARY.

are married, the same men think affection is unnecessary. They think they can skip the preliminaries and move right to the main feature. For many women, however, affection *is* the main feature.

When a man chooses a wife, he promises to remain faithful to her for life. He believes his wife will be his only sexual partner "until death do us part." He makes this commitment because he trusts her to be as sexually interested in him as he is in her. He trusts her to be sexually available to him and to meet his sexual need, just as she trusts him to meet her emotional needs.

But the typical husband ruins his opportunity for a great sexual experience with his wife because he ignores her need for affection.

Although great strides have been made in the last thirty years in the area of premarital sexual counseling and in the development of helpful literature for newly married couples, many men and women still enter marriage sexually unprepared. Men, of course, feel they are very prepared, but being ready for sex and being prepared to make love are two different things.

A man cannot achieve sexual fulfillment in his marriage unless his wife is sexually fulfilled as well. While I have maintained that men need sex more than women, unless a woman joins her husband in the sexual experience, his need for sex remains unmet. Therefore a woman does her husband no favors by sacrificing her body to his sexual advances. He can feel sexually satisfied only when she joins him in the experience of lovemaking.

Since men and women differ so greatly in the way they come to enjoy sex, no wonder we find so much sexual incompatibility in marriage. The key of communication unlocks the doors of ignorance and opens up to each couple the opportunity for sexual compatibility.

The couple willing to learn what they need to know and to practice it together will achieve fulfillment.

COMMUNICATION UNLOCKS THE DOORS OF IGNORANCE AND OPENS UP THE OPPORTUNITY FOR SEXUAL COMPATIBILITY.

Achieving sexual compatibility involves two important steps:

1. *Overcome your sexual ignorance.* A husband and wife must each understand their own sexuality and their own sexual responses.
2. *Communicate your sexual understanding to each other.* A husband and wife must learn how to share what they have learned about their own sexual responses, so that they can each achieve sexual pleasure and fulfillment together.

Many sexual conflicts are resolved when a husband and wife learn what actually happens—emotionally and physiologically—when they make love to each other.

The sexual experience divides into four stages: *arousal, plateau, climax,* and *recovery.* While men and women experience the same four stages, they do not do so in the same physical and emotional ways. What works for a man does not work for a woman, and conversely, what works for a woman does not work for a man. Couples who wish to experience sexual compatibility need to appreciate and understand the differences.

While usually more in touch with their own sexuality because it is such a basic male drive, many men lack skill in lovemaking because they fail to understand a woman's need for affection as part of the sexual process. When a man learns to be affectionate, his lovemaking will become very different. The man interested only in satisfying his hunger for sex molests his wife more than anything else, because his technique is insensitive to her feelings. He uses his wife's body for his own pleasure while she gets more and more infuriated.

Conversely, many women don't understand their own sexuality well enough to know how to enjoy meeting a husband's compelling need

> WIVES SHOULD COMMIT TO LEARNING TO ENJOY THE SEX RELATIONSHIP AS MUCH AS THEIR HUSBANDS DO.

for sex. In order to satisfy her husband sexually a wife must also feel satisfied. I try to encourage wives not to simply make their bodies available on a more regular basis; rather they should commit themselves to learning to enjoy the sex relationship as much as their husbands do.

Obviously, for the wife to enjoy sex she will need help from her husband. If he does not give her the affection and tenderness she needs, she will feel that he is insensitive and uncaring. This principle of reciprocity is applied throughout this book. You can't enjoy your end of a marriage if your spouse doesn't enjoy his or her end. If you care about your spouse, you don't use or deny your spouse out of selfishness or ignorance.

MEET YOUR SPOUSE'S NEEDS AS YOU WOULD WANT YOUR SPOUSE TO MEET YOUR NEEDS.

Almost all cultures and ages know the Golden Rule. Jesus Christ taught us: "Do to others as you would have them do to you" (Luke 6:31). As you think about the concepts presented so far and look ahead to the other eight needs, please consider this slight revision of the Golden Rule: Meet your spouse's needs as you would want your spouse to meet your needs.

Three

CONVERSATION

SHE NEEDS HIM
to TALK to HER

CARING PARTNERS CONVERSE

IN A CARING WAY.

*M*en do not seem to have as great a need for conversation with their wives as women do with their husbands. Women, on the other hand, seem to enjoy conversation for its own sake. Many women will spend hours with each other on the telephone. And meetings, luncheons, and other gatherings where the entire purpose seems to be talking about their personal concerns bring women much pleasure.

Conversation that satisfies a woman's need must focus on the events of *her* day, people *she* may have encountered, and—most of all—*how she feels about them.* She wants *verbal* attention.

Most important, a woman wants to be with someone who—in her perception—cares deeply about her and for her. When she perceives this kind of caring, she feels close to the person with whom she talks. Conversation blends with affection to help the woman feel

SHE WANTS VERBAL ATTENTION.

united with another person. She feels bonded to that person as long as the affection and conversations continue *on a daily basis.*

If a husband seriously wants to meet his wife's need to feel close to him, he will give the task sufficient time and attention. I tell male clients they should learn to set aside fifteen hours a week to give their wives undivided attention.

During courtship, when a couple shares their time, they usually have two basic goals: (1) to get to know each other more thoroughly, and (2) to let each other know how much they care for each other.

The couple desiring a happy marriage carries on with these functions and goals throughout their lifetimes. Primarily for the sake of the woman, they must set aside time to have dates with each other. Here's where my recommended fifteen hours comes in.

A given activity qualifies to be part of the fifteen-hour goal if you can affirmatively answer the question "Does this activity allow us to focus primarily on each other?"

During courtship women fall in love as a result of the time they spend exchanging conversation and affection. If a couple continues to engage in the activities that brought them together in the first place, their marriage will tend to be a good one.

While conversation does meet an emotional need for women, it also serves other purposes in building a relationship. It helps couples (1) communicate their needs to each other, and (2) learn how to meet each other's needs. When a husband and wife take part in conversation that really communicates this information about their needs, they learn to become more compatible. To start such a conversation, ask what your spouse thinks and feels. Use questions such as these: "What has made you feel good today? What has made you feel bad?" Then let your spouse know what made you feel good today and what made you feel bad.

When you share this kind of information, you will better understand what's going on in your spouse's world and his or her reactions to situations that influence you both.

> WHEN YOU SHARE INFORMATION, YOU BETTER UNDERSTAND YOUR SPOUSE'S WORLD.

How do husbands and wives learn to converse in a way that is enjoyable for both of them? How can they learn to use their tongues to make deposits instead of withdrawals in each other's Love Bank?

First, avoid the enemies of good conversation that make you *withdraw* love units from your Love Bank:

Using conversation to get your way at your spouse's expense. There's nothing wrong with asking for what you want from each other. But don't let your requests turn into demands.

Using conversation to punish each other. If you feel angry and resentful, express your feelings by describing your expectations to your spouse. But don't ever use verbal punishment.

Using conversation to force agreement to your way of thinking. Never force your spouse to agree with you. Learn to respect your spouse's opinion and try to better understand its background.

Dwelling on mistakes, past or present. Most people resent denunciations, criticism, or corrections. But if someone we care for explains that he or she would like us to meet a personal need, we are usually willing to help.

Second, consider the friends of good conversation, which help you *deposit* love units into your Love Bank:

Developing interest in each other's favorite topics of conversation. Many people need to begin their conversation with subjects that "prime the pump." Once under way, they can switch to less stimulating subjects and enjoy keeping their end of the conversation.

Balancing the conversation. Be sensitive to each other's right to "have the floor." It may take your spouse two or three seconds to begin a sentence, but allow whatever time is necessary. Also, remember to wait until your spouse completes a thought before commenting on it.

Using conversation to inform, investigate, and understand your spouse. Inform each other of your personal interests and activities. *Investigate* each other's personal feelings and attitudes without trying to change each other. And *understand* each other's motivation in life—what makes you happy and sad.

Giving each other undivided attention. The conversation a woman needs from her husband requires his undivided attention. Set aside fifteen hours for the purpose of giving each other their undivided attention.

When you meet your wife's need for conversation, you come to understand each other more clearly and learn what it takes to meet other important needs. That in turn enables you to deposit love units in each other's Love Banks, which creates and sustains romantic love.

Four

RECREATIONAL
COMPANIONSHIP

HE NEEDS HER TO BE
HIS PLAYMATE

THE COUPLE THAT

PLAYS TOGETHER

STAYS TOGETHER.

*B*y nature, men and women often seem to have divergent tastes when it comes to having fun. Men seem to enjoy recreations that involve more risk, more adventure, and more violence than the recreational interests of women.

It is not uncommon for women, when they are single, to join men in pursuing their interests. They find themselves hunting, fishing, playing football, and watching movies they would never have chosen on their own. But after getting married, wives often try to interest their husbands in activities more to their own liking. If their attempts fail, they may encourage their husbands to continue their recreational activities without them.

MEN PLACE SURPRISING IMPORTANCE ON HAVING THEIR WIVES AS RECREATIONAL COMPANIONS.

That practice is very dangerous for a marriage, because men place surprising importance on having their wives as recreational companions. In fact, among the five basic male needs, spending recreational time with his wife is second only to sex for the typical husband.

Some couples have no problem discovering things to do together. Others, however, are at a total loss. They are just too different and, "Besides *he* simply won't give up his bowling team" and, "*She* absolutely must continue her bridge club on Tuesday afternoons."

No problem. Imagine that around each of you is drawn an invisible circle encompassing all your recreational interests and sources of enjoyment. Within each of your circles there are many interests that overlap. These are the activities that please both of you. Once you find these sources of pleasure, you have your overlapping area of interests to pursue together.

You have many overlapping interests.

No one can do everything he or she would like in life. There's just not enough time. Every person's recreational time amounts to making choices that will leave out other opportunities. Why not select those activities you can share?

When a couple draws up their master list of mutually enjoyable activities, there are many surprises. Some couples discover new activities that neither have ever experienced before but that sound enjoyable. Others discover current activities they didn't realize the other person enjoyed.

Sometimes, though, they find that something they are already doing together is unpleasant for one of them. My Policy of Mutual Appeal covers that situation: Engage in only those recreational activities that both you and your spouse can enjoy together.

ENGAGE IN ONLY THOSE RECREATIONAL ACTIVITIES THAT BOTH YOU AND YOUR SPOUSE CAN ENJOY TOGETHER.

That's a tough rule. Not only does it rule out some activities that you may be doing together, but it also rules out all recreational activities that you are doing individually that only one of you enjoys. For example, a husband might have to give up "Monday Night Football" if his wife doesn't enjoy watching it with him.

If you were to find recreational activities that both you and your spouse could enjoy together, just as much as you enjoy your favorite activities now, it will definitely improve your feelings for each other.

You can't do everything. Out of thousands of possible activities, there will probably exist only a few hundred that my wife, Joyce, and I would enjoy thoroughly. And I cannot possibly do all *those* things. Why, then, should I waste my time doing the things my wife finds no pleasure in?

A HUSBAND AND WIFE SHOULD BE BEST FRIENDS.

I believe that a husband and wife should be each other's best friend, and the principle I've introduced in this chapter "forces" that to happen through the sheer amount of time they spend with each other. My policy of "mutual interests only" says a couple cannot engage in most recreational activities unless they share them. The only exception to this rule allows the husband or wife to engage in some activity that helps achieve an important goal that's agreed to with mutual enthusiasm.

When you follow the "mutually appealing activities" rule, you insure the continuation of deposits in your spouse's Love Bank. Some of my best feelings occur when I pursue a favorite recreational goal. If I share it with my wife, I will associate those good feelings with her, and as my love grows for her our marriage becomes strengthened. If I share these emotions with someone else, I will also associate those feelings with that other person. By doing this, I have lost an opportunity to develop love for my spouse and risk developing love for another woman.

Give yourselves time to adjust and to try new pastimes. You may have some difficulty accommodating these changes, but you'll

COUPLES WHO DO THIS MAKE TREMENDOUS GAINS IN COMPATIBILITY.

find your marriage well worth the effort. In my counseling experiences I've found that couples who limit their recreational activities to those they do together make tremendous gains in compatibility. They also deposit scores of love units.

I encourage couples to try to use at least part of their weekly fifteen hours of undivided attention for recreational activities. The only condition that must be met is that the activity cannot prevent a couple from giving each other undivided attention. If a favorite activity is too distracting to qualify, then a couple must schedule time outside their fifteen hours to engage in it together.

The policy that urges us to make our spouses primary recreational companions is not unbearably painful or unrealistic. In fact, it's the policy we followed when we first fell in love with them. Instead, the Policy of Mutual Appeal invites both spouses to a new level of intimacy and enjoyment of each other.

Five

HONESTY
&OPENNESS

SHE NEEDS TO TRUST
HIM TOTALLY

HONESTY IS THE BEST MARRIAGE

INSURANCE POLICY.

A sense of security is the bright golden thread woven through all of a woman's five basic needs. If a husband does not keep up honest and open communication with his wife, he undermines her trust and eventually destroys her security.

To feel secure, a wife must trust her husband to give her accurate information about his past, the present, and the future. If she can't trust the signals he sends (or if he refuses to send any), she has no foundation on which to build a solid relationship. Instead of adjusting to him, she always feels off balance; instead of growing up *with* him, she grows *away* from him.

A SENSE OF SECURITY IS THE BRIGHT GOLDEN THREAD WOVEN THROUGH ALL OF A WOMAN'S BASIC NEEDS.

The wife who can't trust her husband to give her the information she needs also lacks a means of negotiating with him. And negotiation forms an essential building block to the success of any marriage.

Honesty is one of the most important qualities in a successful marriage. When you are married, you must send each other accurate messages and receive accurate responses.

Couples often make the major mistake of feeling one way and responding in another. Husbands and wives often use the expression "Where are you coming from?" to find out how the other feels. If you project that you are "coming from" a particular place, your spouse will aim there with an appropriate accommodation. If in fact you really come from "somewhere else," your mate winds up missing the target, and you both end up frustrated.

> YOUR SPOUSE HAS A RIGHT TO YOUR INNER- MOST THOUGHTS.

Whenever and wherever your mate asks you how you feel, tell the truth. Don't lie out of fear that you will hurt your spouse's feelings (or possibly hurt your own pride). Your mate has a right to your innermost thoughts. He or she should know you better than anyone else in the world—even your parents.

The husband who lies to "protect" his wife is guilty of the worst sort of chauvinism. He views his wife as an emotional basket case, incapable of coping with reality. And subtly—or not so subtly—treating his wife as though she were emotionally unstable becomes a self-fulfilling prophecy. It is a great way to drive her a little bit crazy.

But when a husband tells his wife the truth, he builds her emotional stability. By always being truthful he tells her he knows she can handle it and can change when she must. The truth may be painful at times (and he should strive to deal gently with the truth), but truth helps a woman feel in control, because now she knows what she needs to do to change the situation.

A husband does his wife no favors when he tells "protective" lies to make her feel secure and loved. Eventually exactly the opposite happens. A husband must present himself to his wife as he is. Then she can adjust, negotiate, and draw closer to him.

Many people ask me, "When you say I have to be so open with my spouse, aren't you taking away all my privacy?"

If by *privacy* that person means keeping part of himself or herself hidden, I hold firm to my conviction that this word has no place between a husband and wife. You may find it threatening to think your spouse might have the right to read your mail or go through your purse, but I believe this kind of openness is indispensable for a healthy marriage.

My wife is the one person who needs to know me best, and I need to provide her with all the information—including the warts. Not only must I answer her questions truthfully, but I must avoid "lies of silence" and readily volunteer information as well. In other words, I must share myself with her in every way possible.

We all have our personality quirks, weaknesses, and problems. That's why we must become as open and honest as possible with each other. We need to understand each other so that we can accommodate and adapt to each other.

The typical woman needs the ability to communicate with her husband any time of the day or night in order to sustain this feeling of openness and honesty. Most women will not abuse this privilege by calling their husbands out of important meetings or otherwise interrupting them at work. However the wife must know that she *can* call if she wants to, and she believes that, when she calls, her trust in her husband is confirmed.

In twenty-five years of counseling I have never discovered the perfect marriage. Each partner has faults and weaknesses of one kind or another: a tendency toward depression; low ego strength; the tendency to crack under pressure; irresponsibility; tendencies toward hypochondria, oversensitivity, or perfectionism. The list could go on and on. However no marriage can survive two things: lack of honesty and lack of cooperation.

No MARRIAGE
CAN SURVIVE
LACK OF HONESTY.

When honesty and cooperation exist in a marriage, you have a couple who is willing to share and to build together. They do not need to be secretive or "private." Neither wishes to lie and shade the truth to "protect" the spouse. When you build your marriage on trust, you experience a joyful willingness to share all personal feelings with the one you have chosen for a life partner.

A woman *needs* to trust her husband. Whatever advantage a man may gain in being secretive, closed, or even dishonest, he wins it at the expense of his wife's security and marital fulfillment. She must come to find him predictable; a blending of her mind with his should exist so that she can "read his mind." When a woman reaches that level of trust, she is able to love her husband more fully.

A WOMAN NEEDS TO
TRUST HER HUSBAND.

Six

An Attractive Spouse

HE NEEDS A
GOOD-LOOKING WIFE

ATTRACTIVENESS IS WHAT

YOU DO WITH

WHAT YOU HAVE.

People often challenge me when I list an attractive mate as one of the most important emotional needs. Shouldn't we be looking beyond the surface and into more meaningful human characteristics, such as honesty, trust, and caring? Besides, what if a woman simply doesn't have the equipment?

Beauty, of course, is in the eye of the beholder, and I am not encouraging a wife to try to look like a beauty queen. I simply mean that she should try to look the way her husband likes her to look.

Does that mean a woman must stay eternally young? Of course not, but getting older is not an excuse for

> BEAUTY IS IN THE EYE OF THE BEHOLDER.

gaining weight and dressing poorly. If your husband tells you that your loss of weight would meet one of his most important emotional needs, you must decide if you care enough about your husband to meet his emotional need.

A man with a need for an attractive spouse feels good whenever he looks at his attractive wife. Most men have a need for an attractive wife. They do not appreciate a woman for her inner qualities alone. They also appreciate the way she looks.

Any woman can enhance her attractiveness to her husband. As I counsel women every week, I observe the following major areas that are particularly important in staying or becoming attractive:

Control Your Weight

The truth is that weight control programs work only when they are a way of life, based on the facts of life. All bodies are machines that burn fuel. When the body takes in too much fuel and doesn't burn it off, it stores the fuel in the form of fat. So if you want to avoid getting fat, you must burn all the fuel your body takes in. To lose weight, you must burn even more fuel.

If you have agreed to lose weight, and keep it off, you must

> MOST MEN HAVE A NEED FOR AN ATTRACTIVE WIFE.

create a new lifestyle around diet and exercise, and your spouse should be a part of it. It may mean that he will avoid foods that are not on your diet and join you in an exercise program. When both of you are committed to this new lifestyle, the chances that it will succeed greatly increase.

Use Makeup to Your Best Advantage

Cosmetics have been around since the ancient Egyptian times, and I have seen many women make dramatic improvements in their appearance by using them.

HUSBANDS APPRECIATE AND ENCOURAGE CHANGE IF IT WAS DONE FOR THEM.

Husbands appreciate and encourage the change if their wives have done it for them. Be certain that in addition to being something *you* like, your husband also finds the cosmetic changes attractive. Keep in mind that your objective is meeting *his* need for your physical attractiveness.

Get a Hairstyle He Likes

I don't encourage women to meekly accept a hairstyle that makes them miserable. Certainly they need to enjoy their own looks and feel a sense of attractiveness. If a husband likes something his wife can't tolerate, negotiation is in order. Among the many hairstyles available, I'm certain they can find one on which they can agree.

Hairstyles, like everything else, can create deposits or withdrawals in her husband's Love Bank. If a wife understands her husband's need for an attractive mate, she will work with him to achieve that goal. Chances are great—in my experience—that she will find that her husband is quite reasonable and has fairly good taste.

Clothes Showcase the Woman

Fashions come and go, and in certain years clothing styles range from silly to disastrous. Despite the insistence of some clothes designers to be eternally creative, one rule still seems to prevail: When women's clothing becomes unappealing to most men, it does not stay popular very long.

A woman should pay as much, if not more, attention to her choice of nightgown or pajamas as she does to what she wears in public. When she dresses for bed, she dresses strictly for her husband. Wearing a worn-out nightgown to bed because "nobody will see it" misses an important point: One very special and important person does see it, so why not wear something attractive? Your husband will certainly appreciate it.

BEING ATTRACTIVE MEETS A NEED

For those of you who are still unconvinced that physical attractiveness is a worthy objective, consider what it means to be physically attractive. It simply means that your appearance makes someone feel good. You meet an emotional need by the way you look. People can be attractive in many ways. If physical attractiveness meets an emotional need of your spouse, why ignore it? Why not deposit love units whenever you have a chance?

PEOPLE CAN BE ATTRACTIVE IN MANY WAYS.

Every woman would benefit from evaluating each aspect of the image she projects—her posture, hairstyle, clothing, gestures, makeup, weight, and so forth. She should ask her husband for his honest appraisal and, if possible, consult professionals or trustworthy friends. The woman then should decide where change is needed and set realistic goals for making those changes. For some, the changes might be completed in a week, while for others it could take

A WIFE'S ATTRACTIVENESS IS OFTEN A VITAL INGREDIENT TO THE SUCCESS OF HER MARRIAGE.

years. But in the end, the makeover would have such significance that it would be life-changing—for the better.

A wife's attractiveness if often a vital ingredient to the success of her marriage. When a woman sees the response of her husband to her improved appearance, she knows that she's made the right decision because it has met one of his deep and basic needs. Her account in his Love Bank will get a substantial deposit every time he sees her.

Seven

FINANCIAL SUPPORT

SHE NEEDS
ENOUGH MONEY
TO LIVE
COMFORTABLY

MANY WOMEN NEED TO

HAVE THE CHOICE OF WHETHER OR

NOT TO WORK ONCE THEY HAVE CHILDREN.

*H*umorous anecdotes abound on women who marry men for their money, but my counseling experience has taught me not to treat this tendency as a joke. In truth a woman *does* marry a man for his money.

Most men are willing to marry a woman who expects to be financially supported throughout life. But there aren't many women who would marry men they would need to support forever.

In fact, most wives do not only expect their husbands to work, they also expect them to earn enough to support their families. Time after time I've been told by married women that they resent *having* to work.

However, hard reality for many women today dictates that they must work to help make ends meet even when their children are small. Their husbands simply can't seem to handle the basic monthly bills on their own.

A WOMAN DOES MARRY A MAN FOR HIS MONEY.

Many couples set a standard of living for themselves far higher than they need to be happy. If they would simply reduce their standards of living to a point of comfort, many could avoid husbands working long hours and wives pressured to earn a paycheck. Sometimes this single adjustment will give women the choice of career or homemaking that means so much to them.

If a couple can "bite the bullet" and lower an unrealistic standard of living, that action frees the husband to set realistic economic objectives regarding the family's basic financial needs.

EVERY FAMILY MUST
COME TO GRIPS
WITH WHAT IT
CAN AFFORD.

Every family must come to grips with what it can afford. Some couples look on budgets as a "necessary evil." I like to call a budget a "necessary good," and I recommend it to almost every couple I counsel. I have yet to meet a couple who sometimes didn't want to buy more than they could afford.

A budget helps you discover what a certain quality of life really costs. I recommend three budgets: One to describe what you *need*, one to describe what you *want*, and one to describe what you can *afford*.

The *needs budget* should include the monthly cost of meeting the necessities of your life, items you would be uncomfortable without.

> A BUDGET HELPS YOU DISCOVER WHAT A CERTAIN QUALITY OF LIFE REALLY COSTS.

The *wants budget* includes the cost of meeting all your needs and wants—things that bring special pleasure to your life. It should be realistic, however: No mansions or chauffeur-driven limos if these lie totally out of your price range.

The *affordable budget* begins with your income and should first include the cost of meeting your most important needs. If there's money left over when the cost of meeting all your needs is covered, your most important wants are then included in this budget until your expenses match your income.

To put these budgets in the context of need for financial support, I recommend that only the husband's income be used in the needs budget. In other words, if his income is sufficient to meet the needs of the family, by definition he's met the need for financial support.

Both the husband's and wife's incomes are included in the affordable budget so that it's clear that the wife's income is helping the family improve its quality of life beyond their basic needs. Some women want to work for the challenges of a career; for others it's to escape from the children. But regardless of the reason, if her husband's income supports her basic needs, she's not working to support herself or her family.

And she may decide that she'll have a higher quality of life by *not* working as much. She may not have as much money, but she has more time with her family. I've been amazed by the number of women who feel much better toward their husbands when his income actually goes to pay for her needs and those of the children.

But what happens when his income is not sufficient to pay for needs budget expenses?

I sympathize with the man trapped in this situation. He does the best he can yet cannot meet his wife's emotional need for financial support. Isn't there an answer to this kind of impasse?

If a husband's income is insufficient, he should improve his job skills. While training for this new job, the family may temporarily lower its standard of living, his wife may go to work, or perhaps both adjustments will be made. I have found that women are usually willing to lower their quality of life and go to work to help support the family if it is a *temporary* solution to a financial crisis. In fact, making this kind of temporary sacrifice can often prove to be a powerful builder of rapport and affection in a marriage.

When a husband and wife work together toward a common goal, their spheres of interests are much more likely to overlap, and their conversations will become more interesting to each other. In short, they become a winning team, and players on a winning team usually like and respect one another.

It's possible to live on much less than we do. Almost any family *can* live comfortably on less than they presently spend. Many people think they need things they may not really need. They sometimes become their own worst enemies. They sacrifice the fulfillment of their marital need for financial support by creating a standard of living they cannot meet. Men sometimes work themselves to an early grave providing for living standards that their families can do without. Sometimes we may measure the cost of high living standards in the loss of life's most valuable treasures.

Together you may prove the truth of Harley's Fifth Corollary: When it comes to money and marriage, less may be more.

Eight

DOMESTIC
SUPPORT

HE NEEDS
PEACE
AND QUIET

MEN NEED

DOMESTIC SUPPORT AS

MUCH AS EVER.

*U*nmet emotional needs often trigger fantasies, and the need for domestic support is no exception. Men often fantasize about a home life free of stress and worry. A revolution in male attitudes in housework is supposed to have taken place, with men pitching in to take an equal share of the household chores. But this revolution has not necessarily changed their emotional needs. Many of the men I counsel still tell me in private that they need domestic support as much as ever.

With the advent of so many dual career marriages, the division of domestic responsibilities has become a major source of marital conflict. Changes in our cultural

MEN FANTASIZE ABOUT A HOME LIFE FREE OF STRESS AND WORRY.

values have contributed greatly to the problem, because there is now almost unanimous agreement that both a husband and wife should share these responsibilities, particularly child care. But change in behavior has not kept pace with the change in values.

If household responsibilities are given to whoever is in the mood to do them, nothing will be done. If one spouse demands help from the other, that will also have an unsatisfactory outcome. But if assignment of these tasks can be mutually agreed upon by willing spouses, everything will run smoothly. I would like to propose to you a solution to your conflict. My solution will not only resolve your conflict, but it will meet the need for domestic support.

> CREATE SOLUTIONS THAT TAKE EACH OTHER'S FEELINGS INTO ACCOUNT.

This solution will require you to do something that is essential in solving most conflicts: get organized. It means you must think through your problem carefully and systematically. You will need to write down your objectives and create solutions that take each other's feelings into account. While you may find all of this awkward and terribly "not you," there is no other way. Besides, when you're done, you may find it to be more comfortable than you anticipated.

Step 1: Identify Your Household Responsibilities

Make a list of all of your household responsibilities. Name each responsibility, briefly describe what must be done and when, name the spouse that wants it accomplished, and rate how important is it to that spouse.

Both of you should be satisfied that your list includes all of the housekeeping and child-care responsibilities that you share. You may have as many as a hundred items listed. Just this part of the exercise alone will help you understand what you're up against with regard to the work that you feel must be done.

Step 2: Assume Responsibility for Items That You Would Enjoy Doing or Prefer Yourself

Now make two new lists, one list titled "his responsibilities" and the other titled "her responsibilities." Then select items that you are willing to take full responsibility for, approving each other's selections before they become your final responsibilities.

Now you have three lists: (1) the husband's list of responsibilities, (2) the wife's list of responsibilities, and (3) the list of household responsibilities that are not yet assigned.

Step 3: Assign the Remaining Responsibilities to the One Wanting Each Done the Most

I suggest that the remaining responsibilities be assigned to the person who wants them done the most. It's a reasonable solution, since to do otherwise would force responsibility on the one who doesn't care about them.

By following this procedure, you may decide to change your attitude about some of the responsibilities on your list. When you know that the only way to do something is to do it yourself, you may decide that it doesn't need to be done after all. In fact, you may find that what kept you convinced of its importance was the notion that your spouse was supposed to do it.

Step 4: Meet the Need of Domestic Support by Assuming Responsibilities That Deposit the Most Love Units

You may not be willing to take responsibility for a certain task because, quite frankly, you don't think it needs to be done. But if your spouse thinks it needs to be done, it may be an opportunity for you to meet his or her emotional need for domestic support.

To be sure that your effort is not wasted, add one more piece of information to your lists of tasks. Beside each task write a number indicating how many love units you think would be deposited if your spouse would do that task for you.

Don't waste your time on needs of lesser importance. Put your energy into what deposits the most love units, and ignore tasks that do nothing for your Love Bank.

Your spouse's response to your help should prove whether or not love units are being deposited. If your spouse thanks you when you perform the task

> PUT YOUR ENERGY INTO WHAT DEPOSITS THE MOST LOVE UNITS.

and expresses his or her appreciation with affection, you know you are on the right track. But if your spouse ignores you after you perform one of these tasks, love units are not being deposited for some reason. In that case go back to your spouse's original list of tasks and pick something else to do that has a greater impact.

When creating a plan for division of household responsibilities, depositing the most love units and avoiding their withdrawal should be your guide. Assume household responsibilities that you enthusiastically accept or want accomplished more than your spouse does. Then, to meet your spouse's need for domestic support, perform some of the tasks on your spouse's list of responsibilities that will be appreciated the most. And do them in a way that doesn't withdraw love units from your own Love Bank.

This approach to the division of household responsibilities guarantees your mutual care, especially when you feel like being uncaring. It prevents you from trying to gain at your spouse's expense, and from trying to force your spouse into an unpleasant way of life with you. It points you in a direction that will give you both happiness, fulfillment, and best of all, the feeling of love for each other.

Nine

FAMILY
COMMITMENT

She Needs Him to Be a Good Father

The best husband is a good father.

*D*espite the current trend among many young couples to avoid having children, I still believe that the vast majority of women have a powerful instinct to create a family. Wives want their husbands to take a leadership role in this family and to commit themselves to the moral and educational development of their children. The ideal scenario for a wife is to marry a man whom she can look up to and respect and then have her children grow up to be like their father.

Women seem to know instinctively what we psychologists have discovered in research and practice: A father has a profound influence on his children. My own father exerted a powerful influence on my educational and moral development. This development of my own moral values was extremely important to my mother, and I am certain she gives him a great deal of credit for training me up in the way she wanted me to go.

A FATHER HAS A PROFOUND INFLUENCE ON HIS CHILDREN.

What does a woman really mean when she says she wants her children to "have a good father"? Behind that remark lie expectations of responsibilities she wants him to fulfill. Ironically enough, they often conflict with his need for domestic support, which was just discussed. In order to deal with such a situation, the couple must achieve open communication in two important areas: time and training.

PARENTING TAKES TIME — LOTS OF TIME

In addition to giving his wife fifteen hours of undivided attention and spending about fifty hours making a living, a man also needs to devote time to his family. He can strengthen both his marriage and his ties with his children by developing what I call "Quality Family Time." Quality Family Time is when the family is together for the express purpose of teaching the children the value of cooperation and care for each other.

> YOU MUST ACHIEVE OPEN COMMUNICATION IN TWO AREAS: TIME AND TRAINING.

What should you plan on doing during these hours? Consider activities such as:

- Meals together as a family
- Going out for walks and bike rides
- Attending religious services
- Conducting family meetings
- Playing board games together
- Attending sports events
- Reading to the children before bedtime
- Helping the children with financial planning

Naturally your list will also include other things you enjoy. Every family has different priorities. Your aim is family togetherness; during this time encourage family members to help each other, showing cooperative spirit. Make it a time for fun with your children, not a time of drudgery. As your children realize Mom and Dad will spend time giving them undivided attention, they begin to look forward to the time.

If you wish to parent your children well, you also need to face the fact that you will need some good training in this skill. No one automatically knows how to care for a child, no matter what the stereotypes may lead you to think.

Look for books that show you some sensible ideas for improving your relationship with your kids. Countless seminars try to explain how to train children. If they stress the parents' respect for the child and show parents ways to improve communication, they, too, may help.

Parent-instruction manuals, books, and courses abound with information on everything from toilet training to enforcing bedtimes.

NO ONE AUTOMATICALLY KNOWS HOW TO CARE FOR A CHILD.

But in regard to a woman's need for a good father for her children, far and away the most significant area any husband needs to work on is learning to discipline children properly. Even more important, he needs to learn how to work with his wife in disciplining children. Some guidelines for fathers follow:

1. **Learn how to be consistent.** Make rules, stick to them, and discipline your children consistently.

2. **Learn how to punish properly.** Be sure to use punishment to help rather than hurt your child. And don't forget the most effective method of discipline: rewards.

3. **Learn how to reach agreement with your wife.** Men must see child training as a joint effort with their wives. Consult together and give agreed upon answers and discipline.

4. **Learn how to interpret the rules.** Children need to understand why they should do this or that. Learn how to clearly and patiently explain the rules.

5. **Learn how to handle anger.** Control your anger before you discipline any child. By separating your emotion from the disciplinary action you will become a more effective parent.

Many men view this need for family commitment as a very demanding role—sometimes too demanding. Because of this, they may neglect the role of father, turning all the parenting over to their wives. By avoiding the role of father, a man loses his wife's respect and the Love Bank account loses out.

On the other hand, men who accept the challenge of good fathering report that they come away with increased marital fulfillment. Their effort comes back to them many times over in the admiration of their wives. As Harley's Ninth Law of Marriage says: The best husband is a good father.

Seek out the books and courses that will make you a better father. Spend time with your children. You'll be glad you did!

Ten

ADMIRATION

HE NEEDS HER
TO BE PROUD
OF HIM

A MAN THRIVES ON

HIS WIFE'S ADMIRATION.

*H*onest admiration is a great motivator for most men. When a woman tells a man she thinks he's wonderful, that inspires him to achieve more. He sees himself as capable of handling new responsibilities and perfecting skills far above those of his present level. That inspiration helps him prepare for the responsibilities of life.

Admiration not only motivates, it also rewards the husband's existing achievements. When she tells him that she appreciates him for what he has done, it gives him more satisfaction than he receives from his paycheck. A woman needs to appreciate her husband for what he already is, not for what he could become, if he lived up to her standards.

ADMIRATION IS A GREAT MOTIVATOR FOR MOST MEN.

For some men—those with fragile self-images—admiration also helps them believe in themselves. Without it these men seem inherently more defensive about their shortcomings.

While criticism causes men to become defensive, admiration energizes and motivates them. A man expects—and needs—his wife to be his most enthusiastic fan. He draws confidence from her support and can usually achieve far more with her encouragement.

How Do You Show Admiration Honestly?

Before you begin heaping words of praise on your spouse, I need to give you a word of caution. Never fake your admiration. By simply saying flattering words to your husband, you can do more harm than good. To have any value, praise must genuinely reflect your feelings.

NEVER FAKE YOUR ADMIRATION.

The first step in learning how to express admiration is to learn how to feel admiration. When you achieve that, you can express these feelings.

You need a plan to help you express true feelings of admiration. That means no word games, nothing phony, only true, honest feelings.

Step 1: Identify Characteristics That Build and Destroy Admiration

A wife must make two lists, the first describing the characteristics she admires in her husband, the second describing those that destroy her admiration. In both lists, she groups these items into the five basic need areas we have already considered for women. Where a characteristic falls out of the areas, she must try to name the need as best she can.

Step 2: Making a Trade

Once you have completed the first step and have listed your strong and weak areas, agree together to overcome the characteristics that destroy admiration for either of you. Ideally, your trade-off should include *all* items you've listed.

Step 3: You Can't Change Traits—You Can Change Habits

As long as you forget about traits and focus on habits, you can change the behavior of your spouse. Often, when we complain about our spouses, we look at their traits not their habits. Yet habits are usually what we really mean and we can do something about them. So your easiest solution will be to define your grievances in terms of habits—then you'll both have something you can measure and evaluate.

Step 4: Learning New Habits

Use this fairly simple and straightforward technique to help people develop new habits: (1) Define the habit you want to create, (2) plan the strategy you will use to develop it, (3) follow the strategy, and (4) evaluate the strategy's effectiveness.

You'll need patience and optimism in your efforts to improve each other's habits. You'll find, though, that even progress can make your marriage so much better that you'll begin to feel the admiration developing.

Tell him, of course! However, that obvious answer is not always as easy as it seems. You may not have learned how to tell your husband you admire him. Just because you *feel* pride or admiration, you have not communicated it. Teach yourself to speak those words of praise, just as you have learned any other habit. Again, remember not to say something contrived or phony. Express honestly how you feel. At first that may seem awkward, but as your habit develops it will become smoother and more spontaneous. Then you'll have achieved your goal: the natural admiration he's always wanted from you.

YOU CAN
BE IRRESISTIBLE
TO YOUR
SPOUSE

*W*hen a husband and wife can't get along, we may describe them as *incompatible*. Yet at one time, we would have called those same two people *irresistible* to each other. Because they found each other irresistible, they made a lifetime commitment in marriage. Couples start out irresistible and only become incompatible as they leave each other's needs unmet.

The quickest cure for incompatibility and fastest road to becoming irresistible lie in meeting each other's most important emotional needs. Happily married couples are already aware of this principle and have learned how to make their marriage a full-time priority. But these couples not only put out the effort, they also put their effort in the *right places*.

THE IRRESISTIBLE SPOUSE

Any husband can make himself irresistible to his wife by learning to meet her five most important emotional needs: affection, conversation, honesty and openness, financial support, and family commitment. Whenever a wife finds a husband who exhibits all five qualities, she will find him irresistible. But if he exhibits only four of them, she will probably experience a void that will nag persistently and incessantly for fulfillment. When it comes to meeting the five basic needs, batting 800 is not good enough. Every husband must try for 1,000.

Similarly a wife makes herself irresistible to her husband by learning to meet *his* five most important emotional needs: sexual fulfillment, recreational companionship, physical attractiveness, domestic support, and admiration. When a man finds a woman who exhibits all five qualities, he will find her irresistible. But again if a wife meets only four of her husband's five emotional needs, he will experience a void that can lead to problems. Like her husband, a wife must seek to bat 1,000 in meeting basic needs.

LOVE NEEDS CONSTANT NURTURE AND CARE.

Few experiences match falling in love. But many couples fail to realize that love needs constant nurture and care. I've tried to give you some guidelines for providing that care and for building a marriage that can become better and better. It takes hard work and a willingness to learn new skills, but when you've done this, you will have mastered one of life's most valuable lessons.

Published by Fleming H. Revell
a division of Baker Book House Company
P.O. Box 6287, Grand Rapids, MI 49516-6287

Printed in Singapore

All material in this book is taken from *His Needs, Her Needs* by Willard F. Harley, Jr.

ISBN 0-8007-7177-X

Cover photo by David Sacks Photography, New York
Design by Christopher Gilbert-Uttley/DouPonce Designworks

For information about all new releases available from Baker Book House, visit our web site:

http://www.bakerbooks.com